Creating Millionaires

How to Sell Your Business/Insurance Agency for Maximum Value and Retire Rich

Mel Clemmons

Creating Millionaires

Published by:
90-Minute Books
Newinformation Inc
302 Martinique Drive
Winter Haven, FL 33884
www.90minutebooks.com

ISBN-13: 9781516862245
ISBN-10: 1516862244

For more information on 90-Minute Books including finding out how you can publish your own lead generating book, visit www.90minutebook.com or call (863) 318-0464

Here's What's Inside…

Marietta, GA
June 2015

A lot of people I come across are experts at knowing how to effectively run and grow their businesses, because they've spent the last 30 years becoming the best business owners in their industry. When they go to sell their business however, they really aren't qualified and don't have the expertise on how to evaluate their agency to determine fair market value. For most of my clients this will be the only business they will ever sell, so it makes perfect sense that selling and evaluating businesses is not one of their core competencies.

I've been sharing these concepts on how to sell your business/insurance agency for years with my clients but I wanted to put the process down on paper for business and insurance agency owners who want to liquidate or retire their business. After reading this book you will know the process and steps you need to take have a successful sale. You'll know all the important things to do like how to position the sale for bank, how to obtain the companies approval in addition to finding the best buyer who will pay maximum value for your agency.

Enjoy the Book!

I hope this book educates you about how to get your business/insurance agency ready for sale and helps change your way of thinking about how you go about selling your agency and encourages you to maximize the sale of your agency and retire a millionaire.

To Your Retirement Success!

Mel Clemmons

Creating Millionaires!

Susan: Good afternoon. This is Susan Austin. I'm excited to be here with Mel Clemmons. Mel is going to be sharing with us his thoughts and ideas on how to sell your business/insurance agency for maximum value and retire rich. Welcome, Mel.

Mel: Welcome. Thank you for hosting today Susan.

Susan: Why did you want to write a book about helping owners sell their business/insurance agencies?

Mel: I'll share a story with you. At one point in time, one of the carriers that we were representing in the insurance field was terminating a lot of people's contracts. These were people who had been in the business for 30 to 40 years. These were great insurance agents, great business owners, but they had no clue about how to liquidate their assets or how to retire, and now they had 90 days to get out of the business. Being self-employed, we often wonder what's going to happen once we retire. We're great at running our businesses, we're great at doing our day-to-day operations, but at some point in time, we're going to have to prepare for the next step in our lives, which is retirement.

As you can imagine, it was a very stressful time for those insurance agents, and it was truly unfair how they were treated by these carriers. I've made it my mission to help other insurance agents avoid the stress and headache that these guys went through when they had to sell under those circumstances. In all honesty, though, most business owners are unprepared for what to do when they go to sell.

Susan: Wow, that's horrible.

Mel: Yes, and that's the number one reason I got into consulting. I didn't like to see people selling under duress. I saw firsthand the impact when someone loses what took them 34 years to build. A lot of them did not know then how to properly evaluate what their businesses were worth, and the carriers were taking advantage of them. I'm the only person in this process who gets paid to represent these selling agents. My whole goal is to make them millionaires. I want them to get paid what they are worth, because I get paid when they get paid. That's my incentive for maximizing their value. If they don't get paid, we don't get paid – until we sell their businesses successfully.

Susan: Walk us through what it looks like when they sell the right way, Mel.

Mel: In all of the successful transactions that I've seen from afar, and the ones I've been involved in firsthand, there are a few key elements that are always present. One, they do their research. They know exactly what the market is saying about the insurance field, or their agency. They've made the effort to find out how many people are looking for businesses like theirs. And they've also looked into how much this type of business is worth. Even after they've learned that, they go on to ask, "Okay, this is what the value is. Who are the lenders playing on this field?" There may be someone who is going to come to the table with two or three million dollars in cash, but most people with two or three million dollars in cash are not looking to throw it away. So, the agency owners need to know which banks are lending to buyers who could buy their businesses.

Besides finding out what a business is worth, a successful agent also takes the time to find out what the process is for selling the business. To sell an insurance firm successfully, the agent will have to know the answers to the following questions:

How do I get my carrier to approve my buyer?

How do I identify where the potential buyers are?

How do I know when I've found a good buyer?

When it's done the right way, the agent either hires a professional to show him how to do these things, or he does the research and finds all of this information on his own.

Susan: Have you seen people who try to sell their businesses on their own? Are they successful?

Mel: It's funny that you mention that. A bank did a study on transactions involving brokers and transactions where brokers were not involved, and found that sellers lose 20% to 25% when they don't have someone guiding them through the process.

One of the reasons that insurance carriers involve me in helping their agents sell their firms is that they know that oftentimes buyers and sellers are emotionally attached to a business. One of the things I've learned about business over the years is not to get emotionally attached. Even though the business might have been in the family for 30 to 40 years, there's no emotional attachment for the person acquiring it. It's a business transaction. I step in and teach people how to separate their emotions from the business transaction. It's not always easy, but it's imperative that they understand how to not involve their emotions. When they're emotionally attached, problems arise. They need to consider what's good for buyers and what's good for sellers, and then find a happy medium. A lot of times, that doesn't happen when sellers try to handle sales on their own.

A lot of business owners might think they have the knowledge and the skills needed to sell their businesses, but there's a reason why there are professionals who sell houses, sell businesses, or sell airplanes. That's what they've been trained to do. Business owners are trained to run their businesses every day, not to evaluate the terms and negotiate with buyers, and not to market their businesses for maximum value. I hate to see people lose money.

Susan: Especially when something like their businesses that they've had for 30-plus years is at stake.

Mel: People want to retire on their own terms. I often tell a potential seller that the key is that even if no broker or consultant is involved, it's a negotiating ploy, because when a buyer knows that a seller has outside guidance or representation, that seller has options. It's similar to selling a house; when the buyer thinks that the seller is acting alone, he or she will just offer anything. But when that buyer knows that someone's been hired to bring in potential buyers, there is a very real threat of somebody else coming to the table, and that buyer could lose out. It creates a different sense of urgency for the buyer, and that works to the seller's advantage.

How to Avoid Killing a Potential Sale

Susan: Why do some deals never make it to the closing table?

Mel: I'll share a few examples of some of the worst deal-killing actions I've seen. First, nothing's in writing. A business owner goes into a huge multimillion-dollar deal, and it's all based on a verbal deal or a handshake. He'll talk to a brother-in-law, who knows this guy who says he'll pay this amount. Trusting someone's word and not getting it in writing can backfire. Second, an owner doesn't ensure that a security deposit was made when it was supposed to be made. And, third, no letter of intent was established, and as a result, there are zero repercussions that would prevent the buyer from just walking away. With no repercussions for that sort of occurrence, the buyer waits, and 90 days down the road, he says, "You know what? Instead of paying $550,000, I've decided to only pay $350,000. Take it or leave it." And this happens on the last day of closing. If there's no contract with built-in repercussions, this can and does happen.

Susan: Have you seen that happen?

Mel: Not on any of the deals I broker, because we make sure the buyer is hit with financial repercussions if there's no closing. So the buyer has the incentive to come to the closing table, and he doesn't hold all the cards.

What happens is that a seller is emotionally attached, but is thinking about retiring, and the day before closing, the buyer changes the terms. That seller is forced to accept the new terms or walk away, and is behind the eight ball in terms of not wanting to take a big loss. In one perfect example that I've seen, the buyer went to the seller and convinced him that the bank approved him only for a certain dollar amount. The seller took him for his word and didn't do a proper investigation, and it cost him $260,000.

Susan: Ouch! So the buyer flat-out lied and said, "This is the best I could do." And that wasn't the case at all?

Mel: I hate to call someone a liar, but he was not forthcoming.

Susan: In your experience, what else might make the sale of an insurance brokerage fall apart?

Mel: Sometimes, in the eagerness to sell, the staff is alerted before the appropriate time. If the staff thinks a sale is happening before it's time to sell, they might get antsy and look for alternative work. So, in the process of trying to sell his or her greatest asset, the seller has key employees leaving. Now, that asset is worth less, because it's missing some key personnel. The buyer will say, "I don't want to buy your business when it's missing key employees." And, when the seller says that the employees quit because they heard the business was being sold, the buyer says, "That's not my problem." So then that seller is stuck with no employees and no buyer.

Susan: Does this happen in real life?

Mel: Yeah, I've actually seen one transaction where the seller actually had an open house before closing to introduce the new buyer. He alerted the employees and sent letters of introduction out to the community, well before the closing date. Then he had no buyer, because the buyer couldn't get financed. That was disastrous for that agency.

Susan: This is like an insider's secret peek behind the curtain at what can go wrong when selling your agency.

Mel: Another mistake that sellers make is alerting the wrong people before a firm deal is made. Before informing the public, a carrier, or the appropriate decision makers, a seller has to make sure to have a conditional letter of agreement. It's important to have certain terms already negotiated, because, when it's on the table, both parties are on the same page. Buyer and seller are one united front.

Another thing that I've seen sellers do wrong is that they look at inaccurate multiples of revenue. They look at the wrong documents. They're trying to evaluate their businesses, but they're not even looking at the proper factors for evaluating businesses.

Four Key Factors to Look at when Evaluating a Business

There are four key factors to look at when you're evaluating an insurance business. Number one is the size of the revenue. That's the most important. How much money is your business bringing in?

The second key factor is retention. How much of your business are you actually retaining on a daily basis?

The third factor is whether or not you are selling ancillary products, such as life insurance, or other products that bring value.

And the fourth factor is to calculate how many losses the business has incurred in a one-year period.

Susan: Is this information easy for owners to access?

Mel: It's easy to access if you know where to look, but the harder part is knowing how to read those reports. If you're not trained in how to read them, then that can be a detriment. You have to be trained to read the reports correctly, or have somebody else read and explain them.

Susan: Is there a formula for using these numbers to help the business owners come up with a value for their business?

Mel: When you sell a business, you either look at the value of the business based on sales or multiple of annual revenue. Business sales are normally based on annual sales or annual net profit. That depends on the shape your agency is in. The better shape it's in, the higher the multiple of your business you can receive.

There are certain people who use a rule of thumb to value a business, but I think that's why they fall into problems. Without digging deep into that business, you don't have a true picture of its worth. A lot of people make the mistake of looking at multiples. The sale of your agency is based on supply and demand. If there's a higher demand for your agency, then your sales price will go up, no matter what multiple you use. If there's not a lot of demand, then you have to be more flexible on price. As with any business, supply and demand is the real key.

Susan: How does someone figure out what the demand is for selling an agency?

Mel: There's been a lot of research on businesses, either using economic data or Federal Labor Department Reports that they can use. Or it can be as simple as looking around in your area to see how many sellers there are. You can also go to your local regional office to tell you how many people are looking to buy in your area, and how many are looking to sell. Or, better yet, you can hire professional researchers that deal with that every day.

Why the Insurance Industry is Booming

Susan: How's the market right now for selling insurance agencies?

Mel: It's the best it's been in the last six years. This is the best it's been in the insurance field in a very long time.

Susan: For selling?

Mel: Yes, for selling. A lot of buyers are waiting in line to buy agencies right now. They want to buy businesses. The reason for this is that there are a lot of baby boomers who have recently retired, and they're looking for something to invest in. You have people who retired at the age of 50 and are not ready to sit home and do nothing. They have money in their 401ks and investments, and they want to look at other opportunities.

There's no other business model similar to the insurance field where you get a guaranteed amount of revenue. Within the last ten years, I've made a lot of people millionaires. The formula is pretty consistent. You can buy a $5,000,000 book for $1,500,000, and then, within 10 years, you use the same cash flow to pay off the loan on the agency. Ten years from now, whether you're 30, 40, or 50, you can put that book on the market when your loan is paid off and now you're a millionaire within ten years. There aren't many other industries that allow you to do that.

How to Prepare to Sell Your Business/Insurance Agency

Susan: How can owners best prepare their agencies to be sold? How far out should they be looking to get ready to sell?

Mel: I usually prepare people to sell three years in advance. When I sell my own businesses - my individual and my family businesses - I'm looking out three years. I like to look down the road so we are never reactive. I always teach people to be proactive when it comes to selling their businesses. But that's not to say that if someone wants to sell in six months, it's too late for them. It's not ideal, but we can make it work. I think that to do it right, it's a three-year plan, because you want to make sure your book is in accurate shape to be on the market. Whether it's a good market or a bad market, you want your agency to stand out.

Susan: What do they need to do to prepare their insurance agency for sale?

Mel: It's really easy. They need to focus on the same four factors I mentioned before. The number one factor is cash flow, which should be at a premium, or how much revenue are they bringing in. They want to make sure that their revenue is at the appropriate level to receive the maximum value when the business sells. If they know their revenue is too low for the business to sell on the open market, or it doesn't cash flow well, they'll want to increase those before they go to sell. Cash flow and net profit should be good. Gross revenue should be good, as well. Sellers need to make sure that their employees, expenses, and revenues are in line to be sold at a good level. They need to make sure the business is really profitable, and they're selling it into profitability. Is it necessary to cut expenses or increase revenue?

Susan: What does the bank need in order to approve the deal?

Mel: The banks are interested in longevity. How long has the seller been in business? The longer you've been in business, the more stable they consider the business. They also want to look at cash flow. They want to see that this book is bringing in this amount of cash for the last five, ten, or however many years. They want to see that it's making money, period. No matter how good the book looks on paper, what's not in cash flow doesn't matter. That means the bank can't get their money if they didn't bring in enough profit. We're looking for good retention, good revenue strings, and not a whole lot of losses or frivolous expenses – no wasting of money.

How to Spot a Good Deal when You Decide to Sell Your Agency

Susan: What are some of the things that someone who is selling an agency needs to know to determine if a deal is good?

Mel: Before he can tell if a deal is good or not, he needs to know how much the market says his agency's worth. How much are agencies in his market selling for? What are they selling for around the country? What was the bank loan on it? What is its evaluation? Is there a previous evaluation? We look at a business just like we do a house. How does a person know if he's getting a good deal on his house? He looks at the value. It's the same thing when he goes to sell his agency. He has to look at the cost, what other agencies have sold for.

If he doesn't have access to that information, he can find the banks that specialize in insurance lending and talk to them to see what their perspective is. Or he can pay for a professional evaluation - that's how it's done. Just like a house. Nobody guesses on the value of a house. Nobody just guesses what a house is worth. They have the house appraised, or pull up the tax records and do some research. Having access to the right resources isn't difficult. The resources are always there. Some people just don't want to pay for that access.

Susan: You have to know how to interpret the data too, though, right?

Mel: Correct. A professional can help with that.

How to Protect Yourself during the Sale

Susan: What should they include in their purchase agreement?

Mel: One key thing to look at and include is tax allocation. How is the deal structured for tax allocations? What is for goodwill? What is for purchase price? What about equipment? Have a tax allocation for tax purposes, so the IRS won't be looking two years from now and saying, "Well, what was this for?" And there's no record to explain things because there's no tax allocation in there.

The second thing is a non-compete clause. What do you plan on doing after retirement? What are you allowed to do?

Next, is there any recourse to come back? Some deals now have seller-financing, where sellers have to carry some financing. Is there access to buy the book back? Is there access to records?

Fourth, who is at fault? What if something was done while the seller owned the agency, and now the new buyers own it? Who is at fault? Who has the liability on that? Those are some of the key factors that should be in the contract. Also, if there's any seller-financing, make sure you're protected, and ensure that it's clear who is responsible for any liabilities that could arise at a certain time.

Susan: A lot of things to consider. When they're negotiating a deal, how they can protect their personal information so that they don't expose too much?

Mel: If I were selling my agency, before I released any information, I would have a non-disclosure agreement or a confidentiality agreement in place. The seller shouldn't share all of his information, because that hurts his leverage while negotiating. If you send every piece of data the person wants and they don't send you a confidentiality agreement, a deposit, or a good faith letter, then you just worked for free to provide all the information they would need to use it against you. When you look at a $1,000,000 or $2,000,000 house, you can't just go walk into that house. You have to show that you have the assets and the net worth to look at it. The same thing applies to an agency sale. They should show how much money they have in the bank, their net worth.

It's like buying a house, some people require a pre-qualification letter. These are things a seller should do to protect himself.

What to Do after Finding a Buyer

Susan: Talk to us about what can go wrong before closing.

Mel: The easy part is getting offers. The important thing is to make sure they give quality offers. One of the things that we have to look at in insurance field is whether the potential buyer has the financial wherewithal to complete the transaction, even though there's a purchase agreement? Do they have the approval of the carrier to take over this agency? Was there a background check? I had one transaction where we, the seller, and the buyer worked together for three months. Two days before closing, the bank did a last-minute background check. The buyer had three defaults on loans, he had a criminal record, so he didn't get approved. That was a bad day for the seller.

When I Grow Up, I am Going to be an Insurance Agent

I know each of us has fond memories from our childhood. For me, there is probably none more significant than that "one day" when I was in the third grade, on the playground, telling my friends that now famous line, "When I grow up, I am going to be an insurance agent." All eyes focused on me intently, and then, to my great surprise, all of the other kids shouted, "Me too!"

With the eagerness all 8-year-olds possess, each of us took turns imagining the day we would get to put on a suit and tie and call prospective clients to try and sell them a universal life policy. All of us were ecstatic about spending our mornings providing a policy review for a family of five drivers, going over liability limits for their auto and homeowners insurance, and discussing the importance of placing their valuable personal property on a policy rider.

Thinking back to that special day opened up even more incredible memories. I remember most of my pals could barely contain themselves just thinking about talking to underwriters about unmatched claims and undisclosed drivers. One of my fellow 8-year-old bud- dies started doing fist pumps over the thought of reviewing an auto policy that resulted in increased premium of $4 per month. Yes, we all agreed, it was going to be a fantastic life as an insurance agent!

In all honesty, that "one day" never occurred, but the embellishment does make our career choice seem a bit more glamorous when viewed through the innocent eyes of an adoring 8-year-old child. Nevertheless, I want to take a few moments to tell you why selling insurance is my chosen profession and why working in our industry is one of the best kept secrets in the business world.

Part of my life's mission is to help 1,000 people become entrepreneurs in the insurance industry. I am unaware of any profession that has so few barriers to beginning a career, yet offers an unbelievable earning potential. In many states, a candidate for an insurance license need only attend a preparatory class lasting as little as a few weeks, take the state exam, and upon achieving a satisfactory score, become a licensed professional. By comparison, lawyers must attend school for about eight years; morticians, about three years; barbers, one-and-a-half years; and television camera operators, about a year of technical school.

Each of these professions mentioned offers the potential for significant in- come, but they also have a limiting factor of not being able to provide a renewable income stream without having to repeat the original effort for which they were compensated.

By contrast, insurance professionals – more specifically insurance agents - have the potential of earning an income stream that could last a lifetime. Through residuals (renewal premiums), insurance agents can out earn virtually any comparable business opportunity. Most people have no idea of the income potential of an insurance agent. While some might frown on the possibility of the general public acquiring such knowledge, I choose to think there is a need to educate more people about the entrepreneurial opportunities in our industry. As agency owners, we are constantly looking for ways to expand our businesses, but without eager professionals to help us grow, we have little to no chance to succeed.

So, how do we change this misconception? A great place to start is with the post-high school education programs offered at many junior colleges or through internship programs offered at major universities. Agents who are willing to mentor aspiring business people can contact either establishment to let them know about opportunities within their agency.

Over the past several years, I have witnessed two "twenty-something" kids, with no formal sales or college education, become multi-millionaires. The first one began his career as a sales producer, and after spending two years learning the ropes, moved out and started his own agency in Stockbridge, Ga. He grew his agency to $3 million in annualized premium within three years. Soon after that, he brought his father into the insurance business and eventually they acquired a large agency. This same young entrepreneur introduced his cousin to insurance and hired him to work in one of his agencies. Thereafter, they purchased or built several more agencies. After all was said and done, their agencies combined annual earned premiums was estimated at $14 million.

The second agent started a scratch agency after being turned down by a few of the large direct writing companies due to his lack of a college degree. His disappointment only left him that much more determined to follow his passion. However, opening the agency did not come without a cost.

Among the many sacrifices he made was having to combine his living space with his office. In addition to this, over the next two years he reinvested virtually all of his earnings into his business. Success followed quickly, and he ultimately hired five sales producers and grew his business into a $4 million agency. He later acquired a $6 million agency, making his agencies net earned premium worth $10 million. He was able to accomplish all of this in just five years. Ultimately, as with most good rags-to-riches stories, he married the woman of his dreams, purchased the home he always wanted, and drives a car most men would sacrifice a body part to own.

Please understand, I am not attempting to use these examples to "rub success in the face of the less successful," but to show the possibilities that result from taking advantage of the leverage our industry provides. Certainly the vast majority of insurance agents earn a more moderate income, but in many cases, this is a limitation of unwillingness to risk capital, combined with a lesser amount of effort. It is not a limitation of the industry.

In the coaching sessions I provide as part of my business, I teach people to believe in the impossible. In certain cases, proving the impossible possible might mean taking a person with no formal training and no college education, giving them a license and a vision, and watching them become a success story for everyone to celebrate. Ultimately in true "pay if forward" fashion, that person would then, in turn, help someone else achieve their dream.

Before I go, I want tell one more story about an agent I know. At 19 years old, in college, with a pregnant girlfriend and no money, this young lad had nowhere to go but up. It was the early 90s, and after a short stint selling cell phones, he was able to secure a job working at a small independent insurance agency. After getting his insurance license, and earning just $7.00 an hour, he soon excelled at insurance sales and ultimately became the agency's sales leader. Soon, this young man helped recruit some of his college buddies, and eventually saw nine of them earn enough to pay their way through school.

Twenty-plus years later, this same "kid" is helping others share the dream of entrepreneurship through his consulting firm.

You can choose to do many things to make money, but what you choose to do in order to make a difference in someone's life will be your legacy.

So far, in this life, I have helped to inspire or create around 57 new business owners. One of those agents who worked for me in college called a few weeks ago from Nashville, TN. He said, "Thank you for showing me the endless possibilities when we were 19-year-old kids." He continued, "I am now a contestant on ABC's new TV show 'Dream Builders,' and I own a construction company that builds multi-million dollar luxury homes."

I thought to myself, 57 down, and 942 more to go, with God's help.

How to Get the Carrier
to Approve the Deal

Susan: What did you mean when you said that the carrier has to approve the deal?

Mel: With a franchise, or somebody who's selling a certain product, the company that owns the franchise or manufactures the product typically has to approve the new purchaser. Let's say someone is selling insurance. The carrier will say, "Okay, you're retiring. Now, Johnny Seed is coming in. We approve Johnny Seed to sell our products." It's the same with say a McDonald's franchise. Even though McDonald's allows someone to sell, they still have a final say-so of who the buyer will be. Any major company is going to have the final say-so about who the buyer will be, because it's their product. The agency owner, or franchise owner, just owns interest in it.

Susan: Do you find that the carriers sometimes don't approve deals?

Mel: Oh yes, definitely. Topnotch carriers who have a high-quality product want to protect their integrity. The deal has to be prepared so the carrier will approve it. It might be the greatest deal, the book might sell for $50,000,000, and the carrier might say, "You know what? This buyer is not the appropriate person. We won't approve this." That deal doesn't go through, no matter how much money is involved. The seller needs to make sure that the person is qualified, and that the carrier is going to approve that person. You need to know what they're looking for.

Susan: What are they looking for?

Mel: That all depends on the company or business being sold. Most carriers are looking for somebody with a good credit score, anywhere from 700 on up. They want to look for somebody who has good experience in sales or in whatever their particular business is. They want somebody with experience. Normally, they want to see five to ten years of experience at a minimum. They also look for somebody who has good standing in the community, whether he's a real estate agent, whether he's a preacher, whether he has community ties. They want somebody who's connected in the community, because that means they have a great ability to sell their product or service.

Why the Lack of a Transition Plan Could Mean Disaster

Susan: What else do they need to know about selling their insurance agency?

Mel: One thing that I've seen happen is that someone is in the process of selling a business, and it's on the market. But he doesn't have a plan in place for what happens if he becomes incapacitated. What happens if he has an accident? What happens if somebody gets sick and can't handle the transaction? In any major corporation, there is succession planning and different transition plans. It's only in the middle market that we don't have access to those products.

Susan: What do you recommend they do?

Mel: There are a lot of companies who offer those products. Procter & Gamble, Ernst & Young and SAMM Consulting all offer succession planning. It's important to have a plan in place that if the key person is not on this planet, or if he is not able to make a decision, what his wishes are? And then, once those wishes are identified, how should they be executed? If the business is specialized, the owner can't just say, "I want my son to run it." If the son/daughter doesn't have experience, he/she can't run the business, and the company won't approve him to run it. So there has to be a plan in place to run it, and the steps he needs to operate the business also need to be spelled out.

Susan: Are you suggesting that these business owners who run multi-million dollar insurance companies don't have succession plans in place?

Mel: Unfortunately, it's true. I would say that 90% to 95% of them have no succession plan in place. Most companies operating with revenues less than $10,000,000 a year do not have succession plans in place, because nobody operates in that field. The big companies that do have succession plans don't have access to those resources. If they do, they get charged $20,000 to $25,000.

Susan: You're saying they have these multi-million dollar assets that they're trying to sell, and if the unthinkable should happen they need to be protected?

Mel: Yes, there needs to be a plan in place. Both buyer and seller need to have a plan in place on how it should be run, or what should happen, if they get sick or – worst case scenario – they should die.

Susan: Have you ever heard or been involved in a sale where someone was incapacitated during the process?

Mel: People have accidents, people get sick, and even before the sale is consummated, e.g. you've had a deal in place and the buyer could say, "You know what? The transition of this business is going to be a lot worse because the owner just died." If, after being in business for 40 years, the owner dies, it's more than likely that there are going to be severe effects on the business.

Susan: Even though he was selling the business, there is negative fallout due to the fact that he isn't there to finish the transition, or there is a negative impact that affects the sale of the business?

Mel: Most people who buy businesses want the former owner, the former employees, or the leader to transition for a period of time, to transition that book off to the new buyer. Whether it's a death or whether it's a transition, they want a transition period for them to introduce you, show you the steps, and explain what they've been doing. Or at least, they want an introduction to the next group of customers who are coming in. Not having a plan in place can really negatively affect the sale of the business.

Why Do I Need Transition Planning?

Gone Too Soon

I remember the ribbon-cutting ceremony for my new office like it was yesterday. I felt like my life had just begun. My wife was there watching, and my parents were so proud of me. My in-laws flew in from out of state and we even had the county commissioner there for a photo op.

Back then, in the beginning, it was just me and a single staff person running the office. I wrote 45 policies my first month, starting with one for a girl who worked at the gas station next to my office. Because I was on enhanced commissions, the money was awesome. I kept writing more and more each month, allowing me to make $100,000 in my first three months. From there, my agency just took off, resulting in award after award. It seemed I was traveling to new countries every other month.

Without realizing it, I had become a successful business owner. I willingly shared my success story with anyone who asked, and eventually, I was invited to speak to new agents all around the country. The company I worked for used my agency as a model for others to mimic, as my phenomenal growth from that of a scratch agency to a $4 million agency proved what hard work could do. I was on a pretty good roll, but what did I forget?

It was also important for me to take care of my family, so I bought life insurance and invested in real estate, both of which were very good decisions in pre- paring for the future. I brought other family members into the business, knowing that my success could be sweeter if the ones I loved also shared in the experience. I was riding high, but I still had a feeling I was missing something. What did I forget?

With my success, also came a level of exuberance that carried over to my personal life. I often told my family members about how I marketed my agency to gain new customers. I stressed the importance of paying your taxes and obtaining a will. Of course, I let them know that if they loved their spouses and children, they had to have life insurance. I wasn't just touting the company line, I truly believed it. But in spite of every- thing I said or did, I still had a strange feeling that something was left undone. What did I forget?

I went to church, and in addition to devoting time to my faith, I was fortunate enough to be able to tithe generously as well as make donations to my favorite charities. I tried to teach my kids that with hard work and a well-thought- out business plan, anything is possible. I constantly showed my wife that she was the most important thing in the world to me by focusing on her, and taking time out "just for us." I was always very busy and yet I tried to never let anything go undone. But still, there was that unanswered question: What did I forget?

Now, I am observing my wife as she looks through a stack of folders. I watch as her fingers dance across the calculator on her desk, as she tries to figure out why there is a deduction from my business account for $8,000 every month. Next, she is asking my employees how much they make each week. She writes out a check for my office lease, but it is not the amount I owe. I want to say something as she progresses through each task, but I cannot.

Soon, the computer guy is there, working on resetting my passwords. This doesn't seem right because I just changed them a few weeks ago, but he proceeds anyway. I see my field sales leader with a letter in his hand. I am not sure what it says, but I watch as my wife takes it and puts it in her pocket.

I can see my staff, but they don't seem to be focused on our customers. Karyn, who is practically a daughter to me, is on monster.com posting a résumé instead of working on the customer contact files on her desk.

My wife is on the phone now, speaking to my CPA. He tells her I owe $35,000 in taxes, but she says she doesn't know which account has enough money to make the payment. He tells her not to worry, and that they can sort it out later. After this, their conversation shifts to the letter that is still in my wife's pocket. She tells him that she has had two offers to buy the agency. She says one of them sounds good because it is for $750,000, which is way above something called TPP. The $750,000 purchase price will be paid over ten years; otherwise they will pay $650,000 cash. The second offer is for less, and the buyer is another agent from the company. My wife says she doesn't know what to do. The CPA tells her she doesn't need the money up- front because of the amount of money the agency has in the bank. Then he cautions her if she does sell, she should be prepared for a big tax bill. I just shake my head. She tells the CPA that the field sales leader says the person offering $750,000 is a great buyer and she should take the offer, especially since time is running out. My wife says "he" had al- ways made these decisions, and that she wished she could have a little more time. I wish I could have had more time, too.

I wish I would have told her that I wanted her to encourage my daughter to get licensed, and become the principal of the agency. I wish I had told her how to calculate the sale price for my agency. I wish I had told her who to trust in trans- acting the sale of the agency. I wish I had written down each employee's salary, or that I gave each of them 10% of their salary as a bonus every February. Sadly, I now realize that I never mentioned any aspect of what I wanted to happen to my agency. So many wishes, but only one big regret. Looking down, I realize I should have done more to make this "after life" transition a lot easier. Unfortunately, I will never be able to fix my regret or answer a single wish, because I was gone too soon.

Why do you need a Death and Transition Plan?

Overlooking a plan for the succession or transition of ownership in single proprietor businesses is more prevalent than it is for larger corporations. In large part, this is because most small business owners are the "face" of their businesses, and are usually engaged in the duteous task of operating them on a day-to-day basis. They never stop and ponder over the "what if scenarios" should they die prematurely.

For many years, I just focused on my business, not realizing that in addition to providing an immediate income, my business also had potentially important and lasting value to those I would leave behind. I knew what I did had purpose, but I completely missed the need to protect the "life" of the very thing that gave me that purpose.

My personal wakeup call was the result of asking myself a rather simple, but obvious, question: "Can I live with the fact that I have done nothing to plan for the transition of ownership for the single largest investment of my life?" If one of your life's goals does not also include a plan for your business to transition after you die, you may need to reassess your goals like I did.

Real life case, with real life consequences

I recently received a call from the spouse of 20-year agent. She told me her husband had passed away, and that he had been an independent agent in Dallas, Texas. She related to me that she was able to determine that he had 20 different contracts with as many different insurance carriers, all while operating as a one-man shop. She didn't know his passwords, phone numbers or names of the representatives of the carriers he represented; she didn't even know how much he received in commissions each month.

It had been two months since he passed away, and because her knowledge of his business operation was limited at best, she assumed that the carriers were handling the customers. By the time we compiled a list of the carriers and client information, her husband's $2 million agency had dwindled down to $700,000 in premium due to customer moves, non-renewals, missed payments, and un-processed endorsements.

The carriers had no idea the agent had died, and because he had never opted for direct deposit, his paper commission checks were just sitting in the mailbox. The outcome for this agent's wife and family could have been markedly different if he had only recognized the need to protect the asset he worked so tirelessly to build.

Four Key elements of a death and transition plan

A death and transition plan does not need to be drawn up by an attorney or a CPA. It is a simple plan that derives much of its information from the things that you do every day – but likely haven't thought about in this context. Its purpose is to provide initial guidance during a time that is filled with emotions and, in many cases, much confusion.

Your plan should include:

- A frequently updated business valuation;

- A plan for your family to follow in order to transition or sell your business;

- A list of key people and resources for your loved ones to utilize after you pass;

- One central location, like a file or notebook, where your survivors can find a listing of all the essential information for your business to continue until proper arrangements are made.

A much-touted statistic is that many attorneys die intestate. With all of their expertise and access to resources, you would think they would know better; yet many of us are just as ill-prepared. It is incumbent on each of us as small business owners, to protect our greatest as- set and to provide our wives and families with the necessary tools to aid them at a time when we cannot. Don't say, "I will do it next month." Don't say, "The company will take care of it." Don't say, "My son will take it over." And don't say, "My spouse will just sell the business." These are selfish, if not foolish, excuses for being lazy. Don't allow your business to be sold at a "fire-sale" price due to your lack of planning. Your next great night's sleep will come after you have completed your own transition plan.

Mistakes People Make when Selling Insurance Agencies

Susan: What are some of the mistakes you've seen people make?

Mel: One of the big mistakes I've seen is when sellers don't trust the professionals they've hired to represent them. I always make the comparison of selling a house. It's just like when you're selling a house, and you're paying a real estate agent to help you sell your house. But you think you know how to sell a house too, so you want to do your own negotiating, you want to do your own marketing. When people walk in, you want to start pointing all the great things about your house and begin negotiations on the spot. If you pay the real estate agent, consultant, or broker to represent you, trust him to do the job. If you hire a lawyer to advise you on your paperwork, trust them to do it.

Don't come in and try to tell them how to do that job. You don't go to the dentist and tell him, "No, I want you to cut my tooth this way. I want you to put this kind of crown on it." But in the insurance industry or when selling a business it happens every day.

Susan: What are some other mistakes you've seen people make?

Mel: Sometimes – and I hate to say this – but sometimes they aren't truthful about their information. For example, the agency owner has known for the past three months that his number one sales agent is about to leave, or that his agency manager is about to quit. However, that's not disclosed before the transaction occurs and that key person just walks out, that seller will look like a liar, which will have a negative impact on your business. It's always better to disclose all information, so everybody can be on the same page.

Another mistake is not having a letter of intent, which should say, "I've seen your initial information. I've met you initially and we've got some background. So if everything keeps looking good, this is what I plan on paying, and this is the time frame I want to do in." Without that letter, everything is up in the air.

A big mistake to avoid is going to the company and saying, "Hey, I'm selling my agency to Susan Smith." But before the transaction is done, Susan Smith changes the terms. The seller has already announced it to the company and they've approved the buyer. So the seller is stuck with making a decision, and has no leverage; or having to going through with a deal that doesn't include the terms he wants; or just backing out of a deal that the company has already approved. The company will say, "I assumed that you had everything negotiated before you came to us, and you had the terms that you expected." They've spent a lot of time working with somebody, and now there's no deal. That's going to create bad will with the company. They're going to think that either you're unprofessional and unprepared, or that you're wasting their time.

Susan: How do you know when it's okay to contact the carrier?

Mel: It's always better to contact the company and let them know the terms, but it should be in writing. The agency owner should let the company that know this is his intention, so when he contacts the company, he'll inform them: "I intend to sell to this person." Or, "I intend to buy this agency." That way, they know to start the paperwork and process the potential buyer.

I would not alert a carrier or a company until I had certain details in place. One of which is, at least, the sales price. Not having an agreed-upon sales price is a pretty big lapse. If the seller doesn't know how much the guy's going to pay – if he's going to pay him for the business – why would he alert the company that he's selling to this person? It's too soon if he lacks that information.

Susan: Are there other mistakes you've seen people make when they go to sell their agencies?

Mel: I've seen a scenario where we had one agent or one businessman who planned on getting back into the business. He didn't want to leave completely, but he signed the contract that stated he would not contact the customers. Little did he know, there was a clause in there stating that he could not indirectly contact the customers. That means if you work for a company that contacts his customers, then he's in violation of his contract. So, he might not ever contact the customer, but if he works for McDonald's and McDonald's sends a newsletter out to one of these customers, he's actually in violation of his contract because it was indirect contact. So, the seller needs to make sure that the lawyers read it closely, because they see this type of language and contracts every day. One word caused him to be in violation of his contract and potentially be sued.

Susan: What else have you seen that has ruined deals?

Mel: I met one guy who was talking to someone about selling his business, and he's giving information and using this guy who isn't in the business of helping people sell their insurance agencies. I told him, "It's just like asking somebody who sells donuts how to sell a house. I don't think you'd do that. I think you'd use a professional, or somebody who actually sells houses." I've seen lot of people take advice from rumors that they heard in the mall, something they read in an email, or something they saw on Yahoo or Google. It doesn't make sense, but people do it.

I think it's sometimes ego, and sometimes they don't see the value in paying a professional or a consultant to assist them. They think they can do it themselves, and they don't see the value in having a professional on their side. But what I've noticed is that most the time, after the transaction, those who use a professional are always pleased, and those who don't really don't know any different, or they look back and say, "You know, I probably could have done better." But sometimes pride and ego say, "Okay, well, I did the best I could." But people don't have to be in that position, because there are a lot of resources that can give them support. My whole focus is on creating millionaires, and so I want to set them up to enjoy the greatest amount of success possible. That's what I specialize in.

Exposing the Myths about Selling an Insurance Agency

Susan: What are some of the myths that are perpetuated in the industry?

Mel: One of the big ones is that a person has to be rich to buy an insurance agency. There are a lot of financial institutions that specialize in new business operators. They have special programs through the SBA and through certain insurance lenders that actually promote people with no experience in insurance, who have either sales experience background, business ownership background, or some type of education that allows them to successfully transfer to the insurance industry. There are a lot of special programs, including special assistance programs that don't even require down payments. There are a lot of myths out there about how much money it takes to buy. Even for those people who are credit challenged, there are ways to go to a financial institute that specializes in short-term loans that enable the prospective buyer to clean up his credit to buy a business.

Another myth is that an agency owner doesn't have control over how or who he sells his business to. As long as he's sitting behind that desk, utilizing resources, and leveraging relationships, he can keep control of who he sells to. He can sell on his own terms. With proper preparation, the seller can always be in the driver's seat, but waiting until the last moment, when he has to react, retire, sell; or the business has depreciated and declined over the last three years, he can't think that it's going to magically turn around to get maximum value when he sells. I wrote an article called *Know When to Hold Them, Know When to Fold Them, and Know When to Walk Away.* And it's the same thing in business. Know when it's time to sell, when it's time to double up and put more money into the business, or when it's time to walk away. You have to know these things.

I hear people say that one location can't merge with another location, which is another myth. They have to realize that there are always exceptions to rules. It often helps to know what the motivating factor is. What is everybody looking for? What does the bank want out of the deal? What does the carrier want out of the deal? What do the buyer and seller want out of the deal? Knowing how to utilize and leverage those relationships to see what everybody wants, can change the rules. There's more flexibility. I've also noticed that, towards the end of the year, when people are trying to hit their bonuses and goals, a lot of people will stretch the rules and make exceptions to fit their own individual needs.

Susan: How does that affect selling a business, though?

Mel: Say for example the carrier's goal is to bring on 50 new business owners by the end of the year.

And they're on 49 and there's 2 weeks left before the end of the year, they will have to bend the rules to hit their target because their bonus is on the line, or they're willing to make an exception. So, the criterion is that they have to have $75,000 liquid, and the buyer only has $35,000, but he's able to get the financing to pay the rest. If the company is one goal away from reaching that target, I'm pretty sure that he's going to be taken into consideration. Those are examples of when things happen in favor of one party or the other, but they have to know when and how to leverage those relationships or situations.

Susan: Do a lot of business owners have unrealistic views about what their businesses are worth?

Mel: Yeah. I just talked to one this month. He's looking to sell his business. He looked out on The Internet, and found a company that promised, "Hey, you can sell from this great multiple." He's located in a rural area, where there's not a whole lot of traffic, so there's no demand for his agency or his business. There's not a long list of people wanting to buy where he is selling. He's basing the value of his company on some factors that don't actually correspond to his situation. Sometimes we have unrealistic expectations, and it depends on your time frame. I speak to a lot of agency owners. I tell them that if they want to sell and they're ready to go sooner than later, find that fair value, and find that happy medium. Sell it for what you consider is fair. That's the best place for everybody to make a fair value.

Susan: Can you share with us a story now of someone who you helped become a millionaire?

Mel: One of the greatest success stories that I can reflect upon is about a young lady, a single mother who actually moved here from another country and got an insurance license. She was getting laid off from her job, and she wanted to stay in the insurance field. She heard that there was a broker who helped people get jobs. So she called me to find a new job or to be placed in a new agency. She told me that one day she'd like to buy her own agency, and I asked what her background was. She told me that she'd been doing insurance for six years. One of the bank's qualifications is that a prospective buyer has been working in the insurance industry for at least two years, and they have a special program. So I said, "Well, you know what? I probably could help you find agencies." She said, "I don't have a college degree. I don't have any money in the bank. I've been making $25,000 to $30,000 for the last six years. I'm not able to run a business." When I asked what she did in the agency, she answered, "I ran the agency. I did the sales. I ran the agency by myself with two other people for years." I said, "Well, sounds like you've already run a business " If she would trust me, I could probably take her to the bank and get her a proof of financing, take her to the carrier, and sell them on the benefits of taking somebody young and energetic in.

She came up with a credit card that had $20,000 on it. She show this to the company, and was approved. I took her to the bank to get approved for a loan. Her credit score was good. The bank gave her 100% financing. They didn't make her put anything down. She bought an agency, and within three years, she doubled its sales, and she's worth over $900,000 now, if she decided to sell that agency.

Susan: Did she sell it?

MEL: No, she's still running that agency. She had a bonus of $65,000 last year, and the agency brings in over $200,000 a year for her family. And she did it all within 36 months. Every day, I see and help create millionaires.

Susan: What about the flip side? Can you share an example of someone who didn't do it right?

Mel: One of the biggest mistakes I saw was made by a guy who was looking to sell his agency. He wanted to sell it for a certain value. He wanted to sell it for 3.5 times multiple, and we kept telling him that was too high. He kept saying, "No, I'm going to get it." So he waited six months. He never got it, and he never lowered his price. He waited another six months; never got it. He waited about 13 to 15 months, and he thought he had a deal on the table. Right at the same time he had a deal on the table, one of the carriers changed his contract, and they took half of his homeowner insurance customers away. He lost over $300,000 in agency value by waiting to try and get above market value. So when he actually did sell, he had to turn it in to the carrier, because nobody wanted to buy it due to low retention. In the end, he sold it for the lowest value, because he tried to hold on for too long and waited for the market to turn around. That's one of the worst cases I've seen.

To showcase one of my greatest success stories, I'll tell you about one gentleman who was selling his agency and relocating because his mom was sick. He had to leave and go to another state to help his mom long-term. He had been trying to sell his agency for about six months. All the time, he was traveling to see his mother, and he kept worrying. He wanted to sell his agency, but he never could find a buyer. He contacted our firm, and we put his agency up for sale on several websites. We had to go into his agency and make a few key changes, meaning that we had to motivate the staff and change the model incentive plan. They started producing more and grew the agency over the next 90 days. He received an offer immediately when we released it, and it sold for a very good value. He was able to spend the next few years with his family before his mom passed away.

What People Say About SAMM Consulting

Thank you so much for your help in selling my agency.

I was told there was no way I could get the price I wanted or the terms that I required.

Not only did you get me the price I wanted, to have it on my terms and closing in less than 60 days was the icing on the cake. Having the choice of two legitimate, QUALIFIED, buyers in the same week gave me the flexibility to have a voice in choosing who would be servicing my clients and my staff. This was a very important factor to me.

Many people were surprised when they found out I sold my agency. They were even more surprised that I used an outside source to sell. They said: "I had no idea you were selling." Exactly! They didn't know, because that was a condition of my sale. I wanted what I wanted, and didn't want to compromise my operation while entertaining offers that may never materialize. I didn't want to lose my status as a top performer with management while waiting for the "right fit" to come along.

I often used a term when my customers would compare my prices with others, I would say "Sometimes you really do get what you pay for". Mel, I certainly got what I paid for when I listed my agency with you. Thank you again and look forward to our continued relationship.

Sincerely

Peter Mansolillo

I was the Field Vice President for the Southeast Region when we hired Mel Clemmons in Atlanta. I remember first meeting Mel at a new agency owner business meeting. He impressed me with his tremendous knowledge, enthusiasm, his solid marketing plan and his drive to become successful.

Mel was In constant learning mode but always willing to share his processes and what worked for him as well as his agency. He was always thinking outside the box. He also understood the value of hiring, developing and retaining a good staff team. This led us to have Mel teach and lead our regional growth classes for all new agents.

These attributes and his commitment to be a top agent enabled Mel to perform exceptionally and reach the highest levels of recognition in our company. In his first full year, Mel achieved the Rookie of the Year award. He went on to win Honor Rings, National Champions and was Chairman's Recipient several times.

Mel has taken these same characteristics into his new endeavor and is a true professional that is always willing to help others with their success. It was a pleasure and an honor to have him on my team, plus an exceptional return on our investment. I'm confident it would be the same for you and your team.

Tim Plohg

I would like to thank SAMM Consulting and Mel Clemmons for all the assistance that they provided me.

SAMM Consulting was truly a one step process for me. They got me two contracts within the first 30 days!! I tried for months to sell to prospective buyers. The majority of buyers wasted a lot of time. The entire staff was good with follow up & follow through, during the entire process.

I highly recommend them, to any seller. It was amazing how this team made everything smooth. They worked with the buyer and my field sales leader hand in hand to make sure everything was approved. He was worth every penny. He exceeded my expectations.

I have been an agent over 40 years and I gladly refer SAMM CONSULTING to you for the sale of your business.

Sincerely,

Buddy Milton

In 2009, I contracted Mel Clemmons to represent me in the purchase of a troubled Allstate agency in North Georgia.

This agency was declining in commission, retention, and earned premium to the extent that the TPP barely covered the agent's loan. Mel's experience and competence were extremely helpful in guiding my decisions and the structuring of this difficult purchase. He earned my trust, respect, and friendship through this purchase.

A few months back, I once again contracted Mr. Clemmons to represent me in the sale of one of my agencies. Honestly, I expected the process to take several months, and I prepared myself to see offers much less than I desired.

In a brief time, Mel presented me with an offer from an outside buyer that desired to relocate the agency to another city. Soon it became apparent the leadership's approval of the relocation seemed unlikely, but Mel assured me to trust him to provide another suitable buyer. Within weeks, true to his word, Mel introduced me to an existing agent that ultimately purchased the agency for a multiple of 2.5!

As the CEO and Partner in six corporations, I rarely provide recommendations and certainly do not offer them flippantly. However; whether you are purchasing or selling an agency, I highly recommend Mr. Clemmons and SAMM Consulting to represent your next transaction. Once you have experienced Mel, you will see why he is well respected for his knowledge, experience and Influence.

Sincerely,

Bruce A. Thompson
Agency Owner & CEO

How to Sell a Business/Insurance Agency for Maximum Value and Retire Rich

Susan: Very nice. If someone has questions about selling his agency, how could he get in touch with you?

Mel: It's easy: Just call the SAMM Consulting office at 678-223-7397. Also, if someone wants to learn more, they can go to the website, www.sammconsulting.com. We have agencies listed for sale, and there is more information about what we do. You can apply online for a free consultation, which we call our Agency Readiness Assessment, where we actually sit down with you before you even contract us. The Assessment helps us see how ready you are for selling your agency.

Our process works like this: After the seller does his research, and contacts us to say, yes, he's ready to work for us, we gather all of the reports to evaluate a true snapshot of the agency. We'll put your documentation in a database, and it'll spit out a form that shows what the agency looks like. This will show what the agency is worth; this is where the money goes in and out. We present that to a buyer. Before we present it to a buyer, the seller contracts us as a consultant, and we sign him up on the consultant agreement, which says, "If we sell your agency, we get paid. If we don't sell your agency, you don't owe us anything." The only thing that we ask is that when we call a client – normally, our calls are worth a couple million dollars – so he will want to pick up the phone when we call, because we usually have a buyer. So that's it. And the only thing I tell him is to get his fishing pole ready, because he'll show up at closing, he'll get a wire transaction, and then he'll be retired. And that's the only thing that we ask.

In the insurance field, we have reports that'll show how many customers an agency has, how much money it's bringing in, and expenses. We'll call that a customer satisfaction report. We'll also ask for a P&L, a commission statement, and a termination agreement. Those are the four forms that we require to get started to properly evaluate your agency for sale. And then once we get close to closing, we'll need tax records, because the bank will want to see the last three years' tax returns before they approve the loan.

There's a reason why clients throughout the country call us for advice on buying and selling insurance agencies. We're the premier consultants because we deal with them on a day-to-day basis. Plus, the people that they'll talk to at SAMM Consulting are insurance consultants. So, when they look for somebody to advise them, make sure they're of the same background. Not only are they consultants, everybody in our office is an insurance agent, so they actually ran businesses, too. They know exactly what a seller is looking for.

Susan: I want to thank you because there's that old saying, begin with the end in mind. I think there is a lot of information out there about how to start or run a company, but not a lot of information on how to successfully sell your business down the road.

Mel: I like to look at running a business as a marathon. There's an end game. It's good to make a lot of money, it's good to want to work for 30 years, but people open up businesses because they don't want to be employed by someone else. They want to run a business and have an end game – we tell them how to retire, how to liquidate assets, and retire as millionaires.

Agency Readiness Assessment

855-306-8627

Agency Readiness Assessment
(AR Assessment)

Circle the answer which is most true for you
TOTAL_____

1. I understand how to make my business data look great on paper for a bank.

Yes: 10 points

No: 0 points

Score: _____

2. I know the market value of my business.

Yes: 10 points

No: 0 points

Score: _____

3. I understand what it takes to get our carrier to approve a new buyer.

True: 10 points

False: 0 points

Score: _____

4. I know what the market conditions currently are for buyers and sellers.

Yes: 10 points

No: 0 points

Score: _____

5. I know how to keep our personal information confidential while selling.

Yes: 10 points

No: 0 points

Score: _____

6. I know the ways and methods to market my agency in order to get offers.

Open: 10 points

Closed 0 points

Score: _____

7. I know how to negotiate the sale to maximize its value.

Yes: 10 points

No: 5 points

Score: _____

8. I know how to recognize a good buyer when presented.

Yes: 10 points

No: 0 points

Score: _____

9. I know how to position my agency in the marketplace for maximum value.

Yes 10 points

No 0 points

Score: _____

10. Because I'm considering selling, I don't need to have a succession plan in place.

Disagree: 10 points

Agree: 0 points

Score: _____

How did you do?

90-100: Your agency is in great shape to sell. Give us a call and schedule a meeting with SAMM CONSULTING to discuss sale details.

80–90: Your agency is doing well; however, there may be a few key areas to improve before you sell. You should call SAMM CONSULTING to discuss.

65–80: There are a few key areas you should address before you sell. You should move quickly to review these areas, in order to maximize when you are ready to sell.

Below 65: Your agency is not ready to be sold just yet. However, you can improve so that you are able to get top value when you are ready to sell. Schedule a meeting with us as soon as possible, so we can help you improve your Agency Readiness Score.

When complete, please email back to **mel@sammconsulting.com**, or Fax to: 678-223-7398.

Name: _____

Company Name: _____

Phone Number: _____

Email Address: _____

Address:

_____

_____

Here's How to Sell Your Business/Insurance Agency for Maximum Value and Retire Rich...

You already know how to grow and run a successful business/insurance agency. The confusing part is knowing how to position your agency when you are ready to sell to maximize the value with buyers, the bank and your carrier.

That's where we come in. We help people just like you sell their business/insurance agency for maximum value without all the headache that a lot of sales bring.

Step 1: Fill out the Agency Readiness Assessment at www.sammconsulting.com and fax back to us at **678-223-7398** or scan and email service@sammconsulting.com.

Step 2: We will review your Agency Readiness Assessment and discuss with you the areas for improvements you can make to get maximum value for your agency.

Step 3: We take it from here and work with you to get the key factors in place so you can get maximum value. This includes what you need to do to attract the best buyer for your agency and how to showcase the sale get bank and carrier approval so you can be assured of a great ending to your career.

Most people greatly underestimate the amount of effort and work it takes to successfully sell their insurance agency.

Now you can sell your business/insurance agency for maximum value and retire rich, all without the headache.

If you'd like us to help, just send an email to: **mel@sammconsulting.com** and we will take it from there.